Albert Krassner

ENCOUNTERS
WITH LOVE

Edited by June C. Groustra

Illustrations and Design
by Ward Flynn

$8.95
ISBN 0-912061-18-9
Copyright 1990 by Albert Krassner
All rights reserved
Veridon Editions, Ltd.
Box 65, Wykagyl Station
New Rochelle, New York 10804
U.S.A.

Printed in the United States of America

Encounters...
like flashes of light in the dark,
sometimes surprising, sometimes expected.
Though limited in appearance
all represent a universal longing
flowing from and to the...
Source

INTRODUCTION

Most of us go through life only briefly and peripherally aware of many of the encounters we have–with places, with things, with sights, with sounds, with people and with God. Most of us simply go on, with little thought to these encounters and their effect on our busy lives. As one reads through the writings of Albert Krassner, it becomes obvious that on his jouney through life, he takes the time to experience and ponder these encounters–recognizing them as exciting and vital, as contributions to a continuing understanding and awareness of a "higher purpose for living." Through his personal strivings and struggles to give greater meaning to life, he has gained a heightened awareness of the excitement and importance of that for which we all strive–*love*.

Gathered by the same substance that gathers it all, these poems form an uneven description of what cannot be described, but has attracted the attention of artists and poets through the times. Let this be an addition to the lovely stream of attempts that precede it.

We hope that you will enjoy the words and graphics in this book. We also hope that as you read these poems you will recall and savor encounters you may have forgotten, and perhaps be encouraged to take a little time to make your future encounters even more meaningful and enjoyable.

June C. Groustra, Editor

Encounters with the flow that always is...
within one's self...
with self in others...
with others and self...
with me, with you, with them...

Encounters with two to become one...
with smile and promise...
with expectation and desire...
with anxiety and release...
Encounters with one through all...

Encounters with what was, will be and is now...
with faith, circumstance and event...
with devotion and ideal...
with care, ease and peace...
Encounters with what is beyond...

Encounters with love...

What is love?
A feeling of being worthy,
A feeling of hope and joy...
An adventure and a journey.
Love is to desire sharing...
Of feelings revealed, fantasies expressed
Shivers of glorious joy
To be seen, felt and accepted.
Love is all around you
Each moment of every day...
Never let go of this feeling,
Live it in every way

Encounters with the flow that always is...
within one's self...
with self in others...
with others and self
with me, with you, with them...

FINITENESS IN ALL
BUT UNIVERSAL LOVE
THERE...IN EVERYTHING

Love overflowing
Ever ongoing
Growing and growing
Contentment knowing

Expressions of self
In whatever form they take
Feeling love flowing

Love will always be

Encounters with the flow that always is...

Love
   An experience
      In daily living

Love
   Beyond all understanding
      The greatest blessing

Love
   When recognized
      Makes life more joyful

Joy in my heart
I feel and know it's there
See it in everyone

Welcome this joy in my heart
Build it in every way
Know that from this very joy

flows peace
flows love

Responding to love
Ever flowing from within
I receive more love

When I am free
Feelings of love flow

How love happens I do not know
All I know is that it is so

Everywhere, everything, forever
Guided by love

Love without a doubt
Flows from inside out

Love is always there
Love is everywhere

9

EACH ONE HIS OWN
AS ONLY HE MAY KNOW
HIS STATE OF TRUE LOVE

Greatest irony
Seeking love outside oneself
Truly found within

...within one's self...

I'm not ashamed
Nor do I fear
If my love shows
What I hold dear

I'm in love
As never before
This love ever grows
Shows more and more

I feel no shame
Nor will I fall
My heart is true
Love is my all

I will not hide
This love of mine
Love so wonderful
Love so Divine.

Feeling love...
    convey it
Feeling love...
    say it
Feeling love...
    live it
Feeling love...
    give it
Feeling love...
    be it
Feeling love...
    see it in all.

...with self in others...

Love is the word
I try to spread

Love one another,
Showing each other we care

Life with happiness
is loving others while living life

IF YOU OPEN YOUR HEART
LOVE WILL FLOW THROUGH

May I go on and on
Speaking to your heart
Bringing you my love

...with others and self...

LOVE IS EVERYWHERE
EXPRESSED PERSON TO PERSON
WARMING TO BEHOLD

GREETING ANOTHER
WITH RESPECT AND GENTLE LOVE
GREATEST EXPRESSION

Giving love brings pleasure galore
Giving I receive only more
It is endless, everyone knows

I only hope that I may live
Always loving...more to give

EXPRESSIONS OF LOVE
NOURISHING ALL LIVING THINGS
CREATING BEAUTY

The essence of life
Wanting to love and be loved
Regardless of age

...with me, with you, with them...

Bringing love to another
Bringing one ease,
Is there any one thing
Which more does please?

Talking, listening
Whatever it may be,
Conveying, caring,
Love, for all to see

Feelings made glad,
Continue to flow,
Each is aware...
Indeed both know

A love experience
Tried and true...
Expressing love to another
Brings love back to you.

May the love you feel be forever
May the hopes you have be fully realized
May your life be filled with sweet moments
May you experience warmth and gladness

Encounters with two to become one...
with smile and promise...
with expectation and desire...
with anxiety and release...
Encounters with one through all...

In all I hold beautiful
        you are there
In thoughts of love
        you are there
In times when I feel one with God
        you are there

It is nothing I can explain
        you are there
Not my wish to know
        you are there
It is something I feel with all my being
        you are there

Let things remain just as they are
        you are there
Have hopes and yearn to be
        you are there
With you around I love my life
        you are there

Never separate
Never apart
Always attached
Within the heart

Always together
In heart and mind
Thoughts feelings
Intertwined

Encounters with two to become one...

Once aloneness
Filled my soul
It does no longer
We have met

Now we tread on
Each his own path
Apart but in touch
Loving together

I love you
As you are...
I long to be with you
Whenever I can be...
I want to feel your love
However it may come to me...
I want to express my love
This love I feel for you...
I want to be with you

Always

...with smile and promise...

All is complete - nothing missing
when I think of you...
All is serene - nothing disturbs
when I think of you...

Getting together
Just to be
All alone
You and me

Being together
Just for fun
Enjoying each other
One on one

Coming together
To explore
All our love
Always more

Whatever happens
Not to care
A great love
We both share

MAY I AFFECT YOU AS YOU DO ME...
IN MY DREAMS, MY FANTASIES, MY LIFE
MAY I GO FORTH FEELING MORE HOPE,
JOY, LOVE FOR YOU...
IN MY HEART

Come share my world of fancy
Let me share with you my dream
Let me guide you to my heaven
Where true loving reigns supreme

Let me show you what I'm seeing
My imaginings let's view
Help me nurture what I'm feeling
A kind of love I never knew

Come and join me in this wonder
Help me see that I can be
A life of loving enduring
Lasting through eternity

HOW MUCH CLOSER CAN I GET TO YOU?

HOW MUCH MORE CAN I THINK OF YOU?

HOW MUCH MORE CAN I FEEL ABOUT YOU?

HOW MUCH MORE LOVE CAN I GIVE TO YOU?

Feeling your absence
Wishing you were near
Wanting your presence
Always to be here

Wanting you nearby
Available to see
Hoping to please you
As you please me

May you be happy
Wherever you are
Always be with me
Never too far

...with expectation   and desire...

Am I strong enough now
to bring you warmth, love, compassion...
to help you love life?

The time will come
to test what is true
whether to give love
and receive it too

...with anxiety and release...

BEING TOGETHER
FANTASING WHEN APART
ENJOYING MYSELF

LOVE IS ALL AROUND
REINTRODUCING ITSELF
GOING ON ALONE

CONCERNED ABOUT YOU
HOPING THAT YOU LOVE ME TOO
KNOWING I LOVE YOU

Constantly thinking of you
Concerned about your welfare
Questioning my role

Wanting you to be happy
Not knowing my effect
I can only pray

May God grant you happiness
May your wishes be fulfilled
Knowing I love you

Raised in loneliness
With no expressed affection
Seeking love and warmth

Discovering love
Independent of others
Love can stand alone

Love is never this
Love is never that
It can be any thing

Love is never here
Love is never there
It can be any place

Love is never when
Love is never then
It can be any time

Love is never you
Love is never me
It is us together

...Encounters with one through all...

I don't know what will happen
as you stir my soul
I don't care...

I feel myself enraptured
I don't care...

I see myself ever more loving
for this I care.

How to free one's feelings
Allow them to come through
Showing the love
Inside of you

How to express emotions
Not suffer love denied
Letting them go
Not held inside

There is a solution
An easy one
When feeling love
Show love to everyone

Encounters with what was, will be and is now...
with faith, circumstance and event...
with devotion and ideal...
with care, ease and peace...
Encounters with what is beyond.

A spell of love I found
Not in this or that
But in everything around
I found that God,
The Love in this world,
Flows through me

Think of beauty, think of love
These are things worth thinking of
Think of flowers, leaves on a tree
All of nature there to see
Think of sky, the moon and sun
Ever there for everyone
Think of wonders to be found
In heaven, on earth, all around
Think of beauty, think of love
Know that all comes from above

Encounters with what was, will be and is now.

Winds ever blowing
Ever ongoing
Feeling love flowing
Always showing
Ever more knowing
God's love bestowing

...LOVE IS A GIFT OF GOD,
FOR ALL THE WORLD AND ME...

All relationships
All arrangements
Time and place control
There is one exception - God
Always available

Can we expect love from another
unless we first discover
love for Self

Can we expect a love that's true
unless we understand
God's love is for all of us

SEARCHING AND SEARCHING
EVER SEARCHING FOR MORE TRUTHS
THEY ARE INFINITE

Searching and searching
For more ways to express love
Always feeling love

As I search for love
I continually find
I am drawn to God

God does manifest
through the heart
Here God's love
has its start

...with faith, circumstance and event...

Now aware of God
I seek to live in His light
Expressing His love

ONLY ONE PURPOSE...
NO DESIRE BUT FOR THE LORD
TO LOVE AT ALL TIMES

...with devotion and ideal...

Seek love in your heart with devoted prayer
And the love in your heart will grow

Please grant me this
Dear Lord above
Always to share
Your wondrous love

As I go my own way
each day
more of God's love I know

In love with His love
No more can I say
Like no other
His love's here to stay

A relationship
Full of joy and fun
Ever exciting
Like no other one

A rich adventure
Like none before
Having begun
Growing still more

Everything wished for
Has now become true
Happened when
His love came in view

56

I am your servant
I am your love
I am your everything
God above

Please let me serve You
This I implore
You are everything
I adore

Allow me to know You
The best I can
Live my life daily
A spiritual man

Personal prisms
Through which the light of God shines
In the form of Love

WITHOUT ANY FEAR
BELIEVING IN LOVE OF GOD
I FIND PEACE WITHIN

...with care, ease and peace...

Ever more aware
How to return to freedom
From negative thoughts

Seeing myself caught
In thoughts of sorrow and fear
I seek peace within

Peace, love lie within
Identifying with God
Happiness returns

I have so much
I want much more...

more to love,
more to give,
more Light to see,
a heart of joy,
more Love for my Lord

It is now here, always clear...
Whenever I think of God
I feel love.

His love is there
Be open to it
Love is in the heart
Always bright
Never dim
Feel His love

Love is limited
by time, space, constant change
when it involves another...

Love is unlimited
when it flows
from and toward God...

Love is wondrous
at all times, in all forms
when expressed.

GOING ON WITH LOVE
RECOGNIZING ITS TRUE SOURCE
BEYOND SPACE AND MIND

...Encounters with what is beyond...

The Divine Presence is inside one's heart,
I know this to be so
God's presence is the love we feel,
A love which yearns to grow

It is not that I have seen a miracle,
Or heard a voice proclaim
I have been made aware of an unbounded love,
To this awareness I lay claim

God is Love, I believe this for me,
I now know it is so
I want to love with all my heart,
Always His love to show

God's love is in everything,
In everyone around
I long to be in touch with Him,
His love in me abounds

God's presence is the sum of all
Of which I am a part
I will try to nurture this love in me
Flowing from my heart

...Do not think that God is only in your heart
You should be able to recognize Him in every garden,
in every forest,
in every house,
and in every person.

You should be able to see Him in your destination,
in all stages of your journey,
and in all your fellow pilgrims.

You should be able to see Him on every path,
in every philosophy,
and in every group.

You should be able to see Him in all acts,
in all deeds,
in all thoughts and feelings,
and in all expressions of them.

You should be able to recognize Him
not only in inner lights,
but also in the lights that you see
in the outer world.

All colors
and even the darkness are the same Being
if you really love Him,
if you want to find His love
and be blessed by it,
then see Him in every corner of the universe.

Muktananda